Service

Starts With a Smile

69 Reasons Why Customers Return

By: Cary Cavitt
PGA Professional
Author, Speaker & Founder of
Service that Attracts Seminars TM
Visit us at www.carycavittconsulting.com

Every customer service campaign must focus on this central point:

"In the final analysis, customers are either won or lost by how much we care about them."

- Cary Cavitt

Table of Contents

Customers will return if you

#1   Learn to smile more…   2
#2   Have a manager who listens well…   4
#3   Sincerely listen to complaints…   6
#4   Simply ask if you would enjoy being served by you…   8
#5   Show enthusiasm…   10
#6   Put away the magazine…   12
#7   Make them feel welcomed…   14
#8   Hire the right people…   16
#9   Make the work environment enjoyable…   18
#10   Never forget the friendly factor…   20
#11   Show them respect…   22
#12   Give them more than they expected…   24
#13   Show attentiveness…   26
#14   Allow refunds…   28
#15   Never point the finger…   30
#16   Respond quickly…   32
#17   Remember they have many options…   34
#18   Treat each person as if they were your first…   36
#19   Give them a sense of belonging…   38
#20   Give options…   40
#21   Give your employees a vision…   42
#22   Treat them like guests…   44
#23   Simply go the extra mile…   46
#24   Have a manager with a service mentality…   48
#25   Maintain the two most important formulas…   50
#26   Avoid the worst mistake…   52
#27   Follow the golden rule of management…   54
#28   Have a friendly telephone voice…   56
#29   Understand their true value…   58

#30	Admit your mistake…	60
#31	Never under deliver…	62
#32	Pleasantly surprise them…	64
#33	Return telephone messages quickly…	66
#34	Desire to be your best…	68
#35	Learn from other companies…	70
#36	Remember to say thank you…	72
#37	Treat everyone the same…	74
#38	Freely apologize…	76
#39	Never ever argue…	78
#40	Strive to WOW them…	80
#41	Make doing business incredibly easy…	82
#42	Remember that they are your advertisers…	84
#43	Learn to trust them…	86
#44	Allow policies to benefit them…	88
#45	Learn to take care of complaints…	90
#46	Remember names…	92
#47	Learn from them…	94
#48	Have a leader who encourages…	96
#49	Understand that laughter attracts…	98
#50	Make them feel special…	100
#51	Learn from customer service superstars…	102
#52	Simply give them what they want…	104
#53	Take care of yourself…	106
#54	Always be consistent…	108
#55	Have telephone manners…	110
#56	Show them you are happy to see them…	112
#57	Focus on others…	114
#58	Empower your employees…	116
#59	Give something extra…	118
#60	Make the first five minutes count…	120
#61	Care about them…	122
#62	Choose common sense over policies…	124
#63	Handle complaints with empathy…	126
#64	Understand why customers leave…	128
#65	Genuinely like people…	130
#66	Give them value for their money…	132
#67	Make customer service training a routine…	134
#68	Enjoy what you do…	136
#69	Serve from the heart…	138

This book is dedicated to all my friends
who started out as customers.

Introduction

The idea for this customer service book came about by the experiences that I have had during the past 30 years of serving others. I wanted to write a simple guide to help others understand what can help to attract more customers to their organization.

In far too many cases, a company will close simply because they lack friendly service. Their product or service may be a great idea. The advertising campaign may have been right on target. The only missing *(and most important)* link was customer service training. The company failed because they did not understand the need to connect with the customer.

My hope is that you will use these sixty-nine ideas and begin to understand that customers first and foremost want to *feel welcomed and appreciated* before they can be won. Serve them from a caring heart and begin to watch what happens!

Best Regards,
Cary Cavitt –M.A.
www.carycavittconsulting.com

Reason #1
Customers will return if you

Learn to smile more…

Our customers will feel more welcomed and at ease if we simply learn to greet them with a friendly smile.

♥

Have you ever strolled into a place and felt comfortable right away? More than likely you were greeted with a friendly smile by one of the employees who acknowledged you.

It's amazing how a simple smile can make us automatically feel welcomed; yet how often we forget to give this powerful little gesture.

Companies that stress the importance of a smile when greeting others are ahead of their competition. The reason for this is that whenever we create a friendly environment for the customer, he or she will be drawn to return. The simple smile conveys to others that we are happy to see them and they in turn feel welcomed.

This powerful combination is really what customer service is all about. The more that we can make the customer feel comfortable, the more likely he or she will continue to do business with us. So remember to encourage your team to smile!

Reason #2
Customers will return if you

Have a manager who
listens well...

Smart managers encourage team members to openly share great customer service ideas.

♥

Every once in a while we will visit a business and sense that there is something different about the way it is operated. The employees generally are happy about what they are doing and the whole atmosphere feels positive.

More than likely, it is because the manager who oversees the operation has a secret that brings this all about. This secret can create a whole new atmosphere and give employees a great place to work. Here's the secret: The manager LISTENS to employees and allows them to share ideas and suggestions in running the business.

When this happens, employees begin to take ownership and enjoy their jobs more because they now feel that they are being respected and making a positive difference in the organization.

Without listening, the business suffers because valuable information is then withheld that could truly enhance better service. Only the truly great listeners become truly great managers.

Reason #3
Customers will return if you

Sincerely listen to their complaints…

Listen to those who have the courage to show you a better way to serve customers.

♥

I have always thought of customers who voiced their complaints as being our potentially best customers in the future. Here is the reason why. The vast majority of customers with a legitimate complaint will never speak up. They just leave and never return. But those who do bring up a problem in the system can possibly become our best advertisers if we can solve the issue quickly and effectively.

Since these so-called complainers have the courage to speak up, think of them as future vocal advertisers who will also speak loudly about our great service. These customers can show us a better alternative in delivering exceptional service if we will take the time to listen to them.

Remember that it is up to us on how well we manage these complaints. Do it right, and we may possibly win a loyal customer who will not be shy in letting others know about our great service!

Reason #4
Customers will return if you

Simply ask yourself if you would enjoy being served by you...

Would you want to be served by you?

♥

Here is a simple question to measure our customer skills: Would you want to be served by you if you were the potential customer? If the answer is yes, then congratulations! But if you answered no, then consider ways to make others happy to be served by you.

When we can put ourselves in another person's shoes and sincerely ask ourselves if we have served him or her to our best ability, then more than likely we would enjoy being served by ourselves.

Consider the excellent customer service experiences that you have had in the past and try to pass on the memorable service to your customers.

In the end, when we simply ask ourselves if we would enjoy being served in the same manner, we can begin to improve and give others great customer service.

Reason #5
Customers will return if you

Are enthusiastic…

Enthusiasm tends to drawn customers in because it awakens a desire to be more excited about life.

♥

There is something attractive about people who are enthusiastic about life. This is especially true when an organization is excited about what they are doing.

Customers will feel this. The pleasure of enjoying work and understanding the allure of enthusiasm will draw others in with curiosity. This is because people are attracted to others who are enthused about life. They see something that they want.

Inside we want to have a purpose that goes beyond our own wants and needs. What we can discover is that capturing a heart of servitude opens a new window of opportunity and makes us more enthused about life.

The most enthusiastic people are those who look outside of themselves and genuinely care about others. When this type of attitude surrounds an organization, others will soon be drawn because they will sense that we do care about them.

Reason #6
Customers will return if you

Put away the magazine...

Reading on the job tells our customers that we do not want to be disturbed.

♥

I am convinced that billions of sales revenue are lost every year simply because an employee is preoccupied and not attentive to the customer.

This on-the-clock employee can easily be recognized as the worker who is sitting reading a book or magazine in the presence of potential customers.

I am always amazed when visiting the local mall and seeing clerk after clerk preoccupied with a book or cell phone, or just playing a game on the internet as customers roam about.

Without realizing it, customers perceive this gesture as a sign of *not wanting to be disturbed.* So instead of inquiring about a certain product or asking for help, the majority of customers just walk away.

If customer service is to prevail, books, magazines, cell phones, and playing internet games should never be allowed during working hours. Having this simple rule will do wonders in providing excellent service and a higher sales volume.

Reason #7
Customers will return if you

Make them feel welcomed...

When an organization shows itself to be friendly and welcoming, customers will be drawn to return.

♥

I believe that the number one factor in drawing people back as repeat customers is based on how well that *they feel* that they were treated. Notice that I said how they feel.

In the majority of cases, most companies honestly believe that they do an excellent job at making each customer feel welcomed. But in reality this is not the case. Very rarely do we come across an organization that truly goes the extra step in making sure that our experience during a visit is outstanding.

Far too often I have left an establishment with a mental note not to return in the near future. I believe that many customers feel this way simply because they did not feel welcomed and appreciated for taking the time to visit the company.

So remember that the key to customers coming back is to treat them with kindness and a friendly welcome.

Reason #8
Customers will return if you

Hire the right people...

During the interview ask questions that will help to determine whether the candidate enjoys helping others.

♥

Finding the right people for the team is the key to ultimate success. But how do we find the best candidate during the interviewing process? Here are two quick tips to watch for:

1. **Watch for great smiles.** Make sure that the candidate can easily smile. I recently went to a local school to volunteer to interview 8th graders who were being trained in writing resumes and interviewing techniques. After interviewing nine students, I chose the first candidate because of his easy- going smile. I felt right away that if he could easily smile in an interview, he could easily smile with customers as well.

2. **Do they enjoy serving others?** This is really the key. Be sure to get a sense of whether or not the possible candidate has a heart to serve. By asking the right questions and really listening to the responses, we should be able to get a fairly accurate reading into whether or not the candidate enjoys helping others.

Reason #9
Customers will return if you

Make the work environment enjoyable...

Happy employees make happy customers.

♥

As I have grown in my understanding of customer relationships, I have also come to realize that the smart companies see each employee as their best customer.

Why have I come to this conclusion? It's really quite simple: *Happy employees make happy customers.*

When management works toward making the work environment enjoyable, the employees respond more positively to customers. The whole atmosphere changes for the better.

Gone are the days when managers ruled with an iron fist. The smart managers have the ability to create a team that not only works well together but also laughs together.

Study after study shows that customer service is greatly enhanced when employees enjoy their work environment. This alone will do wonders for your organization!

Reason #10
Customers will return if you

Never forget the friendly factor...

Remember to include the friendly factor formula when training your employees.

♥

Giving outstanding customer service can be summed up in creating a team that is always friendly to each customer. This is because being friendly *always attracts others.*

Even though this concept may sound elementary, having the friendly factor at an organization must to be continually expressed during employee training meetings.

I believe that the reason friendliness attracts potential customers is because everyone wants to be treated with kindness. When we are friendly, others want to come closer. In essence, we become more approachable to others. This in turn makes others *want to do business with us.*

On the other hand, not being as friendly as we could can convey to customers that they are not welcomed. Remember that the organization that understands the power of friendliness will eventually rise to customer service greatness.

Reason #11
Customers will return if you

Show them respect...

Customers will always respond positively when we show them respect.

♥

Have you ever had a customer experience at a business and could not wait to tell others about it? It happens all the time in the life of a customer. We enter an organization and leave with various impressions of our experience.

This is where a company can either shine or be just another run-of-the-mill operation.

Smart companies understand that there is ultimately one shot at winning potentially new customers. The reason is that in today's economy customers have too many choices. Gone are the days when everyone only had one choice in where to buy their groceries, get a haircut, or do their shopping for basic necessities.

In today's world the only way to rise above the flood of competition is to treat customers with appreciation and respect. When we genuinely show others respect, they in turn are drawn in because we have validated their importance. And in the end, isn't everyone important?

Reason #12
Customers will return if you

Give them more than they expected...

Customers will walk away feeling that the experience was outstanding simply because we gave them more.

♥

Every once in a while as customers we receive more than expected. When this occurs we automatically feel that the company that we did business with was fair and trustworthy.

Because "they did not have to do it," we somehow feel obligated to them in a good way. In essence, we appreciate what they did for us that we want to tell others about the experience. What happened in reality is that we feel that the company really cared about us.

Smart companies understand this basic principle. They will always try to go the extra mile in making sure that they exceed their customer's expectations. This alone can have a big impact simply because the vast majority of customers expect average service.

Remember this and you will find new customers knocking on your door in no time. These customers will also be your best advertisers and tell their friends about the exceptional service!

Reason #13
Customers will return if you

Are attentive…

Being attentive always increases sales.

♥

Sales will always increase when employees are attentive to the customer in a non-pushing manner. This is because the customer feels that they are being treated as an important person.

When employees are attentive, they are letting every customer know that they are there for them. This alone has a powerful impact in the decision that the customer has in whether or not to purchase on the spot or in the future.

On the other hand, when an organization is slack in being attentive to others, the company will soon find itself with lower sales. People who take on the role of being a customer expect to be treated with attentiveness. That is one of the major attractions in going shopping. Customers crave the shopping experience simply because others are attentive to them.

So remember this when training your staff. It is a small tip but results in more satisfied customers and better sales for your company.

Reason #14
Customers will return if you

Allow refunds...

Posting a NO REFUNDS sign up only makes customers less receptive to doing business with your company.

♥

We have all come face-to-face with the dreaded NO REFUNDS or ALL SALES FINAL sign hanging near the cash register. This has to go down as one of the worst signs for creating customer loyalty.

Here is the reason why. First of all, customers will more than likely interpret this sign to read something like this:

"WE DO NOT CARE ABOUT
YOUR SATISFACTION"
"YOU REALLY CANNOT TRUST US"
"WE'VE GOT YOUR MONEY NOW!"

Because the sign is usually next to the cash register, customers leave with a negative feeling. People will not return when they feel that they cannot trust the company. They automatically feel uncomfortable about making a purchase.

But on the other hand, when the policy offers refunds, customers will feel more secure. This in turn increases sales and brings people back to your business.

Reason #15
Customers will return if you

Never point the finger...

Customers are not interested in whose fault it is. They simply want the problem resolved in a professional manner.

♥

One of the worst moves to make when confronted with a customer complaint is to point the finger at another person or department in your company as being at fault.

We need to understand that the customer does not care about whose fault it was. He or she simply would like us to fix whatever the issue may be. To blame another person makes the whole organization appear unorganized in the eyes of the customer.

To them you are the person who represents the company and it is you that they have addressed to fix the problem. The smart move is to simply apologize and do whatever it takes to mend the problem.

Remember that customers are not really interested in whose fault it is. They just want the issue resolved in a quick and professional manner.

Reason #16
Customers will return if you

Respond quickly...

Working quickly during peak customer hours will convey to them that we respect their time.

♥

As customers, we all want to be served quickly. No one wants to wait for very long. This is especially true when lines begin to form. All we have to do is look at the faces. No one seems to be very happy waiting.

It is important that customers see that we are working quickly to take care of them as they are patiently waiting. When customers see that we are going as quickly as possible, it gives them the perception that we truly care.

This alone will give them a favorable impression when they are finally served and leaving the store. Inside they know that it is not our fault and appreciate the fact that we did our best to serve them.

On the other hand, I have witnessed the opposite effect where an employee did not appear to work quickly as others were patiently waiting. This gave the impression that the customer was not important. This attitude will eventually have a negative effect on whether customers decide to return in the future.

Reason #17
Customers will return if you

Remember that they have many options…

Providing excellent service becomes more important when we realize that customers have many options.

♥

Gone are the days when the town had only one barber or one donut shop. In the world of today the customer is given many options to choose from. If he does not like this particular store, he can take his pick from five other local stores. If another customer did not have an enjoyable experience at the new restaurant in town, she has nine similar restaurants to choose from.

This is why it is absolutely critical to win new customers by giving them the best service possible. Other businesses may be able to match our quality and price on the product we may be selling, but if we can have the best service in town it will be hard to lose customers.

As a company it is important for everyone to remember that customers have many choices. If we can keep this in the back of our mind, we can focus more on giving outstanding service. And remember, customers are doing us a favor by walking through our doors when in fact they could have easily did business elsewhere.

Reason #18
Customers will return if you

Treat each person as if they were your first...

A great way to make each customer feel special is to think of him or her as being your first customer of the day.

♥

It is important to train those who work with customers to always remember to treat them as if they were the first customer of the day.

This is because the customer actually thinks this. They never consider that we may have already served ninety-two customers so far on this particular day. To them, they really do not take into account that we may have had a long day and are ready to go home.

The smart companies train their employees to look at every new customer as being the first customer of the day. By mentally doing this, the customer will receive better service and want to do business with your company in the future.

Our job is to serve each person in a professional and proficient manner. We can fulfill this goal by simply giving our customers the sense that they are our first of the day. This will do wonders in how well they are treated.

Reason #19
Customers will return if you

Give them a sense
of belonging...

Customers will be drawn in when they have felt a sense of belonging.

♥

One driving force that people desire is the need to belong. This is especially important in the area of making people feel welcomed and comfortable at your organization.

When a customer is given a warm welcome and feels accepted, he or she will sense that others care. This alone has a powerful effect on how others perceive your business.

They will want to tell others about your company because they trust you and feel that people sincerely care. If we can simply remember that everyone wants to feel accepted, we can then focus on developing a more welcoming atmosphere for our customers.

This sincere heart of consideration for others will make a big difference. In the end they will remember how you made them feel and become your greatest advertisers!

Reason #20
Customers will return if you

Give options...

Allowing your customers many options will give them a more positive and enjoyable experience.

♥

The ultimate goal of customer service should be to give every customer a positive experience. This in turn creates loyalty and free advertising as the happy customer tells others about your great service. This is why it is important to give customers options in order to meet their immediate needs.

Case in point. How many times have you been to a restaurant and have asked to substitute fries for something else only to be told that no substitutes are allowed? This is a simple example but shows how something as mundane as this request can ultimately turn away a potential repeat customer.

Our job in the service industry is to make our customers enjoy themselves and want to come back. The goal should be to give them what they want instead of what we think they want.

Give customers options and they will not only appreciate you for it but will also want to support your business in the future.

Reason #21
Customers will return if you

Give your employees a vision...

Every job should have a greater purpose than simply receiving a paycheck.

♥

What is the best way to develop a great winning team? Simply give them a vision! Everyone on the team needs to see a purpose in what they are trying to accomplish on a daily basis.

Think of some of the great visionaries of the past who had a driving purpose. Thomas Edison was relentless in his pursuit of every invention that he worked on. In a similar way we need to give every employee a purpose and vision that goes beyond just working for a paycheck.

Help your team to see things from a different perspective. Show them that their job is ultimately helping other people to live better lives. It is important that we help them catch a vision of how their jobs are important to others.

People will enjoy their work much more when a leader can get everyone to envision a greater purpose than just holding a job. This new attitude will work wonders in creating a more positive atmosphere and in providing outstanding service to others.

Reason #22
Customers will return if you

Treat them like guests…

Treating our customers as guests will enhance our overall operation.

♥

A great thought for enhancing our customer service experience is to think of every customer who walks through our door as a guest.

Think of it in this way. How do we treat guests when they visit our home? It should be the same way when people visit our business. They have taken the time out of their busy schedule and we in turn should show our appreciation by honoring them in the same manner we would if guests were visiting us.

By seeing customers in this manner, you and your staff will begin to treat them a little more special and be more attentive to their needs. In the long run, the customer will sense this and feel more welcomed and valued.

Remember this simple tip in helping your staff to see each person who walks through your door as a special guest. It will do wonders in how customers are treated and bring them back in the near future.

Reason #23
Customers will return if you

Simply go the extra mile...

Most customers will be pleasantly surprised when we offer great service that was not expected.

♥

On the most part, customers enter a business and expect average service. This is just a fact. They expect the service to be just the normal run of the mill.

The expectations of an average customer are actually quite low when it comes to being served at an organization. The reason for this is because they have had so many experiences with average to below average service that they actually expect it from others.

This of course is a big advantage for your company if you understand this simple point. Your customers will be pleasantly surprised when you give them just a little extra service.

They will be totally caught off guard by your kindness and sincere desire to help them. They will walk away and want to tell others about their great experience.

Reason #24
Customers will return if you

Have a manager with a service mentality…

The best managers reflect their belief in providing great customer service by their words and actions.

♥

In many cases customer service can be a reflection of the management of a company. Managers can either have a great service mentality or miss the boat when it comes to understanding the importance of taking care of the customer.

If the management really believes that customer service is the key to a successful business, it will be reflected in continual training programs. On the other hand, when customer service training is virtually absent, it can be a sign that management does not understand the value of great service.

To be a star manager, it is vital to continually show the importance of customer service by our actions. What are we reflecting by the words that we use and the training that is provided?

In the final analysis, it is paramount that we continually remind our team of the importance of taking care of each and every customer.

Reason #25
Customers will return if you

Maintain the two most important formulas...

We must always be reminded during training sessions to welcome and respect our customers.

♥

In order to build customer loyalty there are two important steps that must be continually maintained in every organization:

#1 *WELCOME THEM*
Every successful business continually creates a welcoming atmosphere. This is accomplished by hiring the right employees who understand the power of kindness. Customers will sense right away that an organization is friendly and happy to serve them.

#2 *RESPECT*
The second ingredient is to give each customer genuine respect. This is just good old-fashioned common sense. Giving proper attention and showing a sincere interest in each customer can accomplish this.

When these two ingredients are present, we will find people being more attracted to our organization and telling others about the great service provided.

Reason #26
Customers will return if you

Avoid the worst mistake…

The worst service mistake is to allow untrained employees out on the floor with customers.

♥

Without question, I have found the worst mistake that organizations can make in regards to providing super customer service is to place an untrained employee on the floor with customers.

Each of us have encountered this. We come to a business and are being served by someone who does not show a friendly greeting or the common courtesy that goes along with the position.

The untrained employee is simply going through the motions without direction. This is not good for business, because customers will soon recognize that this employee does not have the information being asked for or is giving poor service.

More than likely the customer will decide to take his or her business elsewhere simply because of the poor service provided. Is the untrained employee or the management at fault? I think we know the answer.

Reason #27
Customers will return if you

Follow the golden rule of management...

Great managers always follow the golden rule of management.

♥

Great managers all have a similar attribute that separates them from the pack. It is called the golden rule of management:

"Treat every employee the way you want every employee to treat the customer."

The smart manager first and foremost creates an environment where each person in the organization can grow as a person. A manager who sincerely cares for others and shows it in his or her actions shapes the atmosphere.

When employees are treated with respect and encouraged to use their gifts and abilities in an environment of mutual respect, everyone wins and the company begins to thrive.

This simple rule will go a long way in building a great team, cheerful employees, and customers who will return.

Reason #28
Customers will return if you

Have a friendly
telephone voice...

*Customers will automatically make a judgment of the service
offered simply by the tone of voice that they hear.*

♥

The very first impression that every caller will make of your company is the tone of voice that is used on the telephone. The words used are not nearly as important as the tone that is heard by the caller.

A negative opinion of the company can be made if the caller senses that the employee who is answering the telephone is not responding to the questions in a friendly tone of voice.

On the other hand, when the employee projects a friendly attitude and reflects a patient tone of voice to the caller, the caller will have a positive opinion of the organization.

Remember that showing patience and a friendly tone of voice will draw customers in and give them a great first impression of your overall operation. This alone will have a great influence on whether or not they will do business in the future.

Reason #29
Customers will return if you

Understand their true value…

Every customer who enters our door is first and foremost a person who deserves to be treated with respect.

♥

Every company in existence needs to understand that each customer is of value. I have found this thought to be true whether the customer does business or decides not to do business.

It is important to realize that every customer needs to be treated with consideration and respect at all times. We must never forget that every person is of great value and this alone should be reason enough to treat him or her kindly.

People of integrity understand this. They recognize that every customer is first and foremost a human being who deserves to be treated in a friendly and hospitable manner.

This belief alone is so foundational in developing a great customer service base for any organization. Remember this and you will draw others in because of the benevolence that will be felt.

Reason #30
Customers will return if you

Admit your mistake...

Customer service mistakes are bound to happen. If handled correctly, we can win a customer for life.

♥

The time to really shine and show our true customer service genius is when we make a major flop with a customer. Instead of looking at the mishap as a failure, look at it as a challenge to show our brilliant customer service skills!

Here is what I mean. Let us say that we have made a mistake and blew a customer service moment. Now is the time to humbly admit our mistake and make things right. We now have the opportunity to shine and follow with excellent service.

Remember that customers understand that everyone makes mistakes from time to time. What the customer now wants to see is that we are willing to quickly patch up the hole and make things right.

After we have turned around the admitted mistake and made things right, the vast majority of customers will appreciate the effort and eventually forget about the mistake that was made.

Reason #31
Customers will return if you

Never under deliver...

Never promise something that you cannot deliver to a customer.

♥

A good rule of thumb is to remember to under promise and over deliver. That is why companies will tell us that the package will be delivered in 4-6 weeks.

When we receive it in 3 weeks we are pleasantly surprised with the great service! But if the company promised that the package would arrive in 3 weeks and we did not receive it until the 4th week we would be disappointed with the company and the slow service.

Disney World tends to have the waiting line clocks portray a waiting time that is usually slower than the actual wait time for a particular ride. Let us say that the clock flashes 25 minutes before boarding the Disney ride. When we finally reach the boarding zone we are pleasantly surprised to see that the wait time was only 18 minutes.

What Disney actually did was under promise and over deliver. We walk away feeling that Disney has excellent service. By being conservative in our delivery promise we will allow enough time to meet the expectation of our customer and possibly exceed it.

Reason #32
Customers will return if you

Pleasantly surprise them…

We will always leave a great impression when we pleasantly surprise our customers with exceptional service.

♥

In every service transaction our job is to give customers a feeling that they have received more than expected. This is what I call pleasantly surprising them. The customer did not expect the outstanding service and will walk away surprised by the friendliness shown.

When we give our best, we in essence are conveying to our customers that we are there for them. We express through our actions that we value their business and appreciate them as customers. This will speak volumes and bring them back time and again.

Customers who are provided great service also want to tell their friends about the experience. It is human nature to share unexpected acts of kindness and over the top service. Our customers cannot help but tell the world about their wonderful experience.

When we create a team that continually desires to give their best during customer service transactions, we will soon find new people entering our doors.

Reason #33
Customers will return if you

Return telephone messages quickly...

Give customers a great first impression by promptly returning telephone messages.

♥

How many times have you left a telephone message and did not receive a call back? It happens all the time. For some unexplainable reason returned telephone calls seldom happen in the business world.

When we promptly return a telephone message we are telling the customer that they are important. On the other hand, when a message is not returned it gives the impression that our company does not value customers. We must remember that they took the time to call and leave a message. It is only common courtesy that we honor this by returning their message.

The second reason in returning messages is that it reflects great service. The person who left the message will remember our prompt call back and think highly of the quick response. It will let them know that our company is on the ball and can be dependable in the future. This quick response will always reflect positively and give others a reason to trust us.

Reason #34
Customers will return if you

Desire to be your best...

We will always be at our best when we are serving others.

♥

When everything is said and done, the goal of every customer service campaign is to excel in our area of expertise.

In other words, customer service is simply an extension of being able to be our finest on the job. It is showing others that we are striving to create the best possible environment for each customer and continually want to give the best for our clients. By doing our best to serve others, we become better.

I also believe that we are at our finest when we are in the act of serving others. We bring out the best of who we can be simply by focusing on the needs of others and taking our eyes off of ourselves.

The bottom line in delivering great customer service is simply to be focused on others. It is an extension of wanting to be the best that we can be. In other words, treating others well should reflect our willingness to take our eyes off of ourselves and joyfully serve others.

Reason #35
Customers will return if you

Learn from other Companies...

It is always a pleasure to be served by a customer service superstar.

♥

Recently I had an enjoyable experience with what I would call a customer service superstar. Our family had received a package in the mail that contained specialty coffee from a company in Florida. Neither my wife nor I had purchased the product but had noticed that our credit card statement reflected the purchase.

I then called the company and explained that we did not order the coffee. I explained that someone had used our credit card number. The customer service representative understood completely and informed me that we would be credited a refund on our next card statement and to keep the coffee.

She was very prompt and friendly. I could not believe how quickly she had solved the problem. She did not have to go through three supervisors and keep me on hold for fifteen minutes. This simply amazed me. I thanked her and hung up feeling that I had just had the rare pleasure of dealing with a customer service superstar.

Reason #36
Customers will return if you

Remember to say thank you...

A simple thank you conveys to others that we appreciate their business.

♥

I once heard a story about a young man who was fired from an ice cream parlor simply because he continually forgot to say thank you to customers who purchased an ice cream cone.

These two simple words will go a long way in helping to produce outstanding customer service. We can think of this kind gesture as being the closing to any customer service contact. A friendly thank you will always leave customers with a positive reflection of the service that was provided. When customers hear a thank you, they immediately feel appreciated.

These two powerful words also will tell customers that you think highly that they have done business with your company. On the other hand, when a customer walks away without a thank you, they have an inner feeling of not being appreciated. This alone can have an impact on whether or not they will want to do business with your company in the future.

Reason #37
Customers will return if you

Treat everyone
the same...

Every person who makes contact with our organization must be treated with appreciation and respect.

♥

In every business there are really only two types of people who will walk through our doors. The first being purchasers. They actually do business with our company and are considered buying customers. They may also continue to do business with us in the future.

The second type of person has not made a purchase but may consider doing so in the future. Both types are important. The reason for this is that every person has the potential to become a loyal customer in the future. It should not matter if a purchase has been made or not.

The important point to remember is that we need to treat every person as a valuable customer who deserves to be warmly welcomed. Since we can never tell who may be a future loyal customer, it is essential to give great service to everyone. This mindset will go a long way in enhancing better service to each person who may enter our doors.

Reason #38
Customers will return if you

Freely apologize...

Customer service mistakes can be handled correctly if we start out with a sincere apologize.

♥

Every customer service person will eventually make a mistake with a customer. It is just a fact of life. We may blow an order or forget something that needed to be done for a customer.

So how do we handle it when we drop the ball? First and foremost we need to apologize for the mistake. This alone will do wonders to calm the situation and let the customer know that you are sincerely sorry for the mistake. The words "I am sorry" shows the customer that you respect them and are admitting a mistake on your part.

The vast majority of customers will accept this kind gesture and quickly show forgiveness. Now it is your turn to make up this mistake by giving them outstanding service. This also will give you a great opportunity to shine and go over the top with service. Not only will the customer appreciate your effort, but may tell others about the mistake and how wonderfully you handled it.

Reason #39
Customers will return if you

Never ever argue...

Showing kindness and patience during a difficult customer transaction will do wonders in calming down the situation.

♥

To argue with a customer is the same as telling them to never come back again. This also gives the customer a reason to advertise negatively about your company. It is a no-win situation.

As customer service people, we will come up against potentially difficult customers who may just be having a bad day. We need to realize that they are not essentially angry with us but may be upset with something totally unrelated to the present moment.

We must not take this personally. If anything, our goal should be to show patience and understanding in this situation. It may also help to reflect back and remember a time when someone had shown us patience and how much we appreciated this kind act.

By showing kindness, we are giving them what they may need at the moment. And in the end, they will walk away and appreciate the patience we displayed when they were not at their best behavior. It is a gift that they did not expect.

Reason #40
Customers will return if you

Strive to WOW them...

Customers who leave with the WOW effect will soon be telling others about the wonderful service provided.

♥

Have you ever walked away from a business and could only describe the service provided as a big WOW? That is the big buzzword being used today in the customer service world.

The WOW effect is nothing more than giving your customers service that they did not expect. It leaves them wondering what just took place. They walk away with the feeling that the service they received went far beyond what was expected.

As customer service providers our goal should be to WOW the customer so that they will walk away wanting to tell others about our wonderful service. They in essence become walking advertisers simply because we offered them caring service. We could say it is going the extra mile in customer service.

Strive for the WOW effect and you will soon see customers returning and telling friends about your wonderful company!

Reason #41
Customers will return if you

Make doing business incredibly easy...

Serving our customers in a quick and efficient manner will always convey that we respect their time.

♥

We all have had the experience of doing business with a company that was incredibly difficult. The transaction process was slow and we left with the feeling of never wanting to do business with them again. One easy way to give great customer service is to provide your customers with a simple and quick way to make a transaction.

Let me share an example that will hit home. Let us say that every time you visit a local restaurant the waitresses are incredibly slow. So what happens? Eventually you find another restaurant.

Great service needs to respect the time of each customer. When a transaction is long and difficult, customers will eventually find another company to do business with.

It is important to train each employee to finish transactions as quickly as possible and give every customer the impression that their time is valuable. They will always leave with an impression that the service was excellent.

Reason #42
Customers will return if you

Remember that they are your advertisers...

Word of mouth will always be our best source for marketing our products and services.

♥

There is one way of marketing your organization that is superior to all the rest. It is free and more convincing than any commercial or print campaign. More people will listen to this type of marketing than to any other advertising strategy. So what is this marketing approach that I am referring too? It is called word of mouth advertising.

There is no better avenue in the world for marketing our business than by having satisfied customers talk about their enjoyable experience. This word of mouth advertising will attract more people than any other campaign. That is why it is so important to strive to give every customer a wonderful experience.

On the other hand, poor service will have the opposite effect in advertising our business. Customers will also tell others about their bad experiences. When this happens we will soon find less people coming through our doors.

The key is to treat every person with great service and eventually see the positive results of happy customers spreading the word.

Reason #43
Customers will return if you

Learn to trust them...

Customers who sense that we trust them will be encouraged to do business with us again in the future.

♥

We need to remember that most customers can be trusted. When making company policies, we need to take a hard look at whether every rule and regulation we have will enhance the service or be a hindrance in attracting customers. Is the policy intended for the few but punish the majority?

Here is an example: It would be like having a security guard walk around a store intimidating every customer with his uniform and suspicious looks. He may distract a few who potentially may steal. But in the long haul this tactic would scare the majority of customers away. Is it really worth making every customer feel uncomfortable simply because of the few who may attempt to steal?

It is important to re-examine policies and ask if they are beneficial for the vast majority of customers. If not, then it may be time to throw them out and find a better system. A simple tip to remember is that if customers sense that we trust them, they in turn will be drawn to return.

Reason #44
Customers will return if you

Allow policies to benefit the customer...

Every new policy that a company makes must ask if it will have a positive effect on the customer.

♥

A question that continually needs to be asked when making company rules is this: How will this benefit the customer? Will this decision enhance the experience for our customers or will it have a negative effect in drawing them back to your business?

I believe that every new idea or change in company procedures must benefit the customer. Every decision must have the customer's best interest at hand.

Change is inevitable. Every day new decisions must be made in regards to running a business. Nothing is wrong with change per se. But the important point to remember if we want to keep customers coming back is to ask how this will benefit their experience.

If the change will be positive, then by all means go for it. But if a decision is being considered that may hinder providing excellent service, it may be worthwhile to re-evaluate the change.

Reason #45
Customers will return if you

Learn how to take care of complaints...

Listening and empathy will go a long way in calming down an upset customer.

♥

Every customer service person will eventually be confronted with an upset customer. There are some positive ways to handle this situation. The most important key is to actively listen to the complaint. Allow the customer to talk. This alone will show that we care.

It is important to maintain a calm voice when replying back if the customer is speaking in a louder than normal voice. Never raise your own voice. In these situations the customer is looking for two responses. The first is simply to be listened to. The complaint may be legitimate and help us in the future so that it is never repeated.

The second response that the customer is looking for is empathy. If we can show that we understand how they feel, we are then giving them a caring response. The upset customer will more than likely calm down simply because we have listened and showed empathy. Now it is our turn to handle the situation in a calm and professional manner.

Reason #46
Customers will return if you

Remember names...

Use the skill of association when remembering names.

♥

It has been said that when a person hears his or her name, it is like fine music to the ears. We all like to be remembered. It especially works wonders with our customers. When we remember names we are telling them that we genuinely care and appreciate their business.

Have you ever been introduced to someone and then came across him or her again in the future. Out of nowhere they call you by name. You are impressed that they have actually remembered it! It is the same when we call our customers by name. They feel welcomed and are impressed that we took the time to remember them.

People who have the gift of remembering names all use the skill of association. This simply means that you associate the name with another person or object that you are already familiar with. If you meet a man named Frank and have a cousin named Frank, you now have an association. Try it and watch customers perk up when they hear their name!

Reason #47
Customers will return if you

Learn from your customers...

We will always have an advantage if we listen to our customers.

♥

Have you ever met someone who loved to ask questions? They were not afraid to seek answers. People who are inquisitive continue to grow because they continue to learn. In the business world it should be the same.

As a business, our goal should be to continue to enhance the experience for our customers. One sure way to improve is to ask questions and listen to them. The reason for this is simple. Customers are seeing the operation from a different point of view. They are on the outside looking in.

What customers see and experience may be completely different from what we may think. In far too many cases, a company may believe that they are providing excellent service but have never asked the opinion of the customer.

We will always be at an advantage if we listen to our customers. Not only will they appreciate that we have heard them, but our service will begin to improve dramatically.

Reason #48
Customers will return if you

Have a leader
who encourages...

Leaders who are in the habit of giving positive reinforcement will encourage their employees to become their best.

♥

There is something different in an organization where the leader continually encourages others. This little secret will do wonders in motivating people to do their absolute best.

We all like to be encouraged. It is no different in the business world. It is a known fact that people will always improve when they are given sincere encouragement. On the other hand, if a leader never provides compliments on a job well done, the team is continually left in the dark on whether or not they are meeting expectations.

Every truly great leader has learned that positive reinforcement will always outperform negative reinforcement. People will give their best if they are encouraged and complimented on a regular basis.

Customers will also sense that something is different and feel the positive attitudes of those who serve them. This positive support then creates a chain reaction that is passed down to the customer.

Reason #49
Customers will return if you

Understand that laughter attracts...

Everyone is attracted to the sound of laughter. Wholesome laughing is both healthy and contagious!

♥

The winning organizations all have a way of making the working environment enjoyable for all. One way to develop this positive work atmosphere is to incorporate laughter.

Everyone is attracted to the sound of laughter. This is no different for every customer who enters our door. When they observe that employees enjoy their work environment, they will be more influenced to return. Companies that take care of their team have learned that happy employees make happy customers.

When people laugh on the job, the atmosphere becomes more enjoyable. Customers will sense this and will walk away with a more positive opinion.

As a business, we must never forget that wholesome laughter has many health benefits and is attractive. Learn to take situations less seriously and try to see the humor in daily life. This little tip will improve customer service and create a friendlier atmosphere.

Reason #50
Customers will return if you

Make them feel special...

People will always gravitate towards those who make them feel special.

♥

As little children, most of us loved to visit our grandparents, because they made us feel special and welcomed. As we grew older the desire for this feeling did not change. People will always gravitate towards places where they feel special.

The smart companies understand that every person is unique and should be treated as such. When we create a team that appreciates this, people will soon gravitate towards our business. This caring connection will give us a huge advantage. In the end, customers will remember how we made them feel.

If your organization has employees who care about others, you will find that customers will continue to be drawn back to your business. Others may be able to match your product and price, but the real advantage will come when you have a team who truly cares about people.

Reason #51
Customers will return if you

Learn from customer service superstars…

We will know that a superstar has served us by their friendliness and the way that they made us feel.

♥

One of the fastest ways to learn how to be a customer service superstar is to observe our own experiences as a customer. Being on the other side of the counter will give us a different perspective.

I love to observe and watch how others treat me as a customer. Every so often I will come across a service superstar. They are courteous, attentive, and make me feel great to have done business with them. These superstars have a way of making me feel welcomed and appreciated.

When we make a conscious effort to observe others, we will begin to recognize certain actions and attitudes that may or may not work.

Remember to keep your eyes open when you come across the superstars. You will recognize them by their smile and the way they make you feel. We can learn a lot from them.

Reason #52
Customers will return if you

Simply give them what they want...

Customers are looking for respect and attentiveness. Give this and the product or service becomes more satisfying.

♥

Great customer service can be summed up in *simply giving customers what they want*. It is finding out what their needs are and then delivering it to them. That is why it is essential that we listen to them.

So what do customers want? The primary desire of every customer is to be treated with respect and attentiveness. They expect to be treated kindly and with consideration. When customer service representatives provide this, customers will feel more satisfied and sense that they are receiving great service.

The product or service being paid for is secondary to the treatment received. When attentiveness and respect are given to the customer, the product then becomes even more satisfying.

We must remember that customers seek a feeling first and the product or service second. Give them courtesy and consideration and they will walk away feeling that your products are the best!

Reason #53
Customers will return if you

Take care of yourself...

To be at our best, be sure to add proper rest with the right diet and exercise.

♥

If we are to be at our best with others it is essential that we take care of ourselves. This involves three important areas in our life.

The first significant area in helping us to be at our best is getting enough rest. More often than not, many of us are not as productive simply because we do not acquire enough sleep. Our performance level will suffer when we are tired.

The second area that can bring out the best in us is having a proper diet. What we eat can be compared to what we put in our gas tank. When we are careful with maintaining a better diet, our "engine" will run at a higher level.

The final area in bringing out our best is maintaining a regular exercise program. This will help us to sustain a higher energy level throughout the day.

We will be at our best when we combine enough rest with a proper diet and a regular exercise program. These three areas will also help to improve our service to others.

Reason #54
Customers will return if you

Are consistent...

Consistency will give our customers a comfort in knowing that they will receive the same service in the future.

♥

Recently I had the pleasure of visiting a new ice cream parlor with my family. The experience was memorable with great ice cream and very friendly service. The servers behind the counter wore a great smile and were very attentive. They were customer service superstars in action.

But this was only part of the overall experience. Everyone in my family ordered a small ice cream cone. When we received the cone the ice cream on top looked like a triple scoop! We were definitely impressed with the amount of ice cream received. As we left I wondered if this experience would be consistent for other customers as well.

I thought that the combination of great service with a great product (forgetting the calories involved!) would make this place the talk of the town. The point of sharing this story is for us to be aware of the importance of being consistent. This consistency will give our customers a comfort in knowing that they will receive the same service or product time and again.

Reason #55
Customers will return if you

Have telephone manners...

Customers will make a judgment on the quality of our service simply by how well they were treated on the telephone.

♥

1. Be sure to answer within three rings to convey your quick service.

2. Cheerfully state your organization and your name to connect to the customer in a more meaningful way.

3. Keep a gracious tone of voice at all times to convey a friendly atmosphere.

4. Listen intently. Stating back to the caller what is being requested conveys a sincere concern in meeting their needs.

5. Always reflect patience. Being patient again conveys friendliness.

6. Always reflect helpfulness. When customers sense that you want to help them they will always respond positively.

7. Always reflect kindness. Being kind will always attract others.

8. State your answers clearly and professionally.

9. Never keep someone on hold for over 30 seconds. Apologizing for the wait conveys that you respect their time.

10. Always close with a friendly "Is there anything else that I may assist you with?" This leaves a great impression that your company desires to meet and exceed the customer's original request.

Reason #56
Customers will return if you

Are genuinely happy to see them...

There is no better feeling of being greeted by someone who is genuinely happy to see us.

♥

There is a secret in providing a great first impression for your customers that works every time. This little secret only works when we mean it from our heart.

So what is this great secret that will win customers? It is being genuinely happy to see them. There is no better feeling of being greeted by someone who is happy to see us. We tend to perk up and feel happy ourselves!

When others are glad to see us we feel a sense of belonging and this in turns makes us feel comfortable. Because the first few minutes are crucial in the experience of a customer, it is important to be consistent in providing a friendly greeting.

All of us enjoy the feeling that others are happy to see us. We long for affirmation and the sense that people care. This will go a long way in giving our customers great service. Being genuinely happy to see them provides a great first impression and a reason to return. Mean it from the heart and watch what happens!

Reason #57
Customers will return if you

Are others-centered...

Life becomes more fulfilling when we focus more on others.

♥

As in the life of each person, every company must ultimately make the decision to focus more on self or others. This one choice will set the course for every path that the organization will eventually follow. The two options are available but can never reside together.

I have found that life is more fulfilling when we live for others. This simply means that living with the goal of servitude gives us more satisfying lives. We discover a greater purpose. To live a life that is focused on others makes life more meaningful and ultimately brings out the best of who we are.

We can learn a lot by studying those who chose to serve others. They should be our models if we are to find greater joy in our lives. Focus on others and see what happens. Not only will we find a more fulfilling life, but customers will also sense a difference in our organization!

Reason #58
Customers will return if you

Empower your employees...

Empowering our employees will eventually bring the best out in them.

♥

What is the easiest way to bring out the best in employees who are out in front serving customers? The most excellent way that I have observed from great managers is that they give them the freedom to make decisions.

Every day frontline employees are put into situations of having to make decisions that will affect the customer being served. In order to be most efficient, employees should be able to resolve the vast majority of issues without having to find a manager.

Nothing is more frustrating for the customer than having to wait for the manager to arrive in order to resolve an issue that could easily have been handled by a frontline employee. This ultimately reflects a company that does not trust employees.

I do believe that in certain cases a manager will have to make a decision but this must never be the norm. In the end it will be freedom and trust that will bring out the best in your employees.

Reason #59
Customers will return if you

Give something extra...

What exactly does your organization offer that makes customers want to come back?

♥

What exactly does your organization have that will make customers want to tell others about your great service? Is there anything different that you provide that makes you shine above others? The answer to these questions can either make or break your success.

I have often thought that if I owned an ice cream parlor I would provide free sprinkles with every purchase. This little gesture would speak volumes to customers. I would stand out above the other parlors simply because I provide free sprinkles. My cost for this service would be minimal. The benefits would far outweigh the investment.

In the same way, we need to find ways that make others want to come to our organization. What can we do differently that will separate us from the others? Find something that will show your customers that you care and they in turn will show you their appreciation by becoming loyal.

Reason #60
Customers will return if you

Make the first five minutes count...

Customers can decide within the first few minutes whether or not to return in the future.

♥

I am convinced that many customers make a decision whether or not to return to a business during the first five minutes of making contact. This is the time that they are making a verdict on how well the service is and whether to return in the future.

If we want new customers to come back it is critical that we give them a great first impression from the start. We need to greet them with a friendly smile and be attentive to their immediate needs. This excellent service during the first five minutes will make a big impression and stay with customers for a long time.

It is also a great reminder to view every new customer as a potential customer for life. New customers are what will keep a company going strong. When they walk through our doors we need to give them a great first impression through excellent service. This not only will surprise them but also give them a solid reason to return again.

Reason #61
Customers will return if you

Care about them…

Great customer service is simply caring about other people.

♥

If I had to tell others what constitutes great customer service I would simply state that caring about other people is the answer. It really does not matter how much training and manuals are written about customer service if the caring factor is not involved.

The reason that caring is the most decisive part in providing excellent service is that customers can tell if we are genuine in helping them. We may follow our customer service policies and do everything we were taught in our training but lose customers simply because they sense that we do not care.

Hopefully this will never be the case, but it is important to remember that customers can tell if an organization truly cares about them and their immediate needs. We continually need to be reminded that people do not care how much we know until they know how much we care. If we sincerely care about others our service to them will be more genuine and easier to perform.

Reason #62
Customers will return if you

Choose common sense over policies...

Having a bundle of red tape can be a major cause in losing customers.

♥

Every organization needs to have company policies and procedures in order to operate. But in far too many cases common sense is lost in the sea of rigid rules. We make policies and leave no room for good old-fashioned common sense.

Having a bundle of red tape in our manuals can be a major cause in losing customers. They decide not to return simply because we cannot make a decision that will benefit them. Our typical answer is that it is "company policy" and if we did it for them we would have to do it for everyone.

The smart companies allow their employees to make decisions that are based on the situation at hand. The goal should be to do whatever it takes to keep a customer.

If employees were given this freedom there would be more happy customers. By allowing common sense to rule we are also putting more confidence in our employees. This in turn will allow them the freedom to perform at their best.

Reason #63
Customers will return if you

Handle complaints with empathy...

We can win customers by offering them empathy and a listening ear.

♥

Customers who complain can be turned into our most loyal fans if we handle them with empathy. The majority can be won over if we listen to them and hear what they have to say.

The dictionary defines empathy as being able to identify and understand another's situation or feelings. When we sincerely listen without making quick judgments we are offering them empathy. Customers will appreciate that we have given them our attention.

Because the vast majority of customers will leave before complaining, the very few who do have a legitimate complaint can help us to better our service. Showing them empathy is the key to making them feel understood.

It is also important to note that just because some customers tend to complain about anything, we must not classify every customer with a complaint in this category. Learning to discern what is truly legitimate will help us to improve in our services to our future customers.

Reason #64
Customers will return if you

Understand why customers leave...

Apathy occurs when we forget that we are in the people business.

♥

The main reason that customers leave and never return is because of apathy. They can sense that an organization does not care about their needs. When this occurs it is hard to win them back.

Apathy is a "disease" that can spread and close the door faster than any other problem being faced. Customers first and foremost want to know that we sincerely care about them and their needs. When this attitude is not felt they will quickly find another company to do business with.

Apathy occurs when we forget that we are in the people business. Our goal must be to see our customers as people who have feelings just like us. And like us, they can tell when customer service is performed as just another obligation in order to get a paycheck.

Customer service is about serving others and enjoying it. We must continually remember that customers are people just like us who long for others who sincerely care.

Reason #65
Customers will return if you

Genuinely like people...

Customers are drawn to places where others naturally show a likeable disposition towards them.

♥

Customer service becomes easy for those who genuinely like people. This is because customer service is about meeting the needs of others. When we like people it becomes easy to serve.

I believe the first qualification for hiring employees is to somehow find out if they like people. This is especially important for employees who will be making daily contact with customers.

The secret in hiring a great service staff is to find people who enjoy being around others. Companies who surround themselves with employees who enjoy people will soon find more customers coming through their doors.

Customers will be attracted to places where others naturally show a likeable disposition towards them. It is human nature to like others who tend to like us. Customers will want to come back because they appreciate the friendliness that was shown to them.

Reason #66
Customers will return if you

Give them value for
their money...

*Providing excellent service at a fair price will give customers a
reason to return.*

♥

Customers as a whole are looking for a value. They appreciate and enjoy the feeling of knowing that they received a good product and service for their money. Providing this combination will give customers a positive reason to return time and again.

Customers cannot help but tell their friends when they are given a great deal with great service included. This is because on the most part they do not expect to be given both at the same time. As customers, we usually think of receiving a fair price with average service. That is why providing excellent service is an additional benefit that was not expected.

Is it possible to give our customers both an excellent value and great service at the same time? Absolutely! This combination will win back customers every time. They will not only be back but will be our best advertisers for bringing in new customers.

Reason #67
Customers will return if you

Make customer service training a routine...

We all need to be reminded from time to time of the importance of taking care of our customers.

♥

Every one of us who provides service to others will routinely need to be reminded of how important it is to take care of our customers. This can be accomplished by making customer service training a regular part of our ongoing education.

Continual training should be a regular part of every organization. This is because it is easy for all of us to forget the most important reason that we are in business. Without customers we would soon have to close our doors.

By having regular training, we are reminding our employees that we are first and foremost in the people business. Our job is to take care of our customers and to make sure that they have an enjoyable experience.

These regular training programs can focus on the various aspects of taking care of customers. The important point to remember is to continually remind our team that customers are our greatest resource.

Reason #68
Customers will return if you

Enjoy what you do...

Our level of enjoyment on the job will help to promote a positive attitude towards our customers.

♥

Employees who enjoy what they do tend to perform at a higher level than those who are less passionate about their job responsibilities. This is especially true for those who provide customer service.

Customers can sense when we take delight in serving them. Our attitude can be felt immediately and leave a positive impression. This can only occur when we enjoy what we do.

The reason that enjoying our job is so important is because it will determine our attitude. Enjoying our work tends to bring about a positive and optimistic attitude. On the other hand, looking at our employment as just a means to a paycheck will effect our attitude and make a difference in how well we treat our customers.

We can develop a positive frame of mind on the job if we look at our position as a way to help others. Our attitude will change for the better and allow us to offer excellent service to our customers.

Reason #69
Customers will return if you

Serve from the heart...

Serving others becomes much easier when we serve from the heart.

♥

I intentionally left what I consider to be the best for last. We can and will always provide excellent service if we serve from the heart. This is because caring must be the central foundation of every customer service campaign.

We can go through the best training, read the best customer service books, and follow our service manuals to the letter. But when it comes down to becoming a customer service superstar, we will never reach our potential until we serve with a caring heart.

Serving from the heart simply means that we genuinely care that each customer is given the best service possible. We ask ourselves how we would like to be treated if we were the customer. We serve with their best interest in mind.

In closing, when it comes to customer service, our primary focus is to see each customer as a person just like us who would like to be treated fairly and with respect. This is serving from the heart.

A closing thought...

I sincerely hope that these thoughts will become a part of your overall training in the future. Every organization should continue to create ways in providing excellent service to their customers.

We are confident that these sixty-nine ideas will give your customers a reason to return and eventually become loyal and tell others about their positive experience. In essence, customer service is about creating an environment where customers *want to return.*

This is why we have created our on-site *Service that Attracts Seminars* TM. The insightful workshops are available for organizations that are looking to motivate their team in providing excellent customer service.

If you would like to learn more please visit our website. We look forward to hearing from you soon.

May you enjoy serving others!
Cary Cavitt
www.carycavittconsulting.com

www.ingramcontent.com/pod-product-compliance
Lightning Source LLC
Chambersburg PA
CBHW020207200326
41521CB00005BA/282